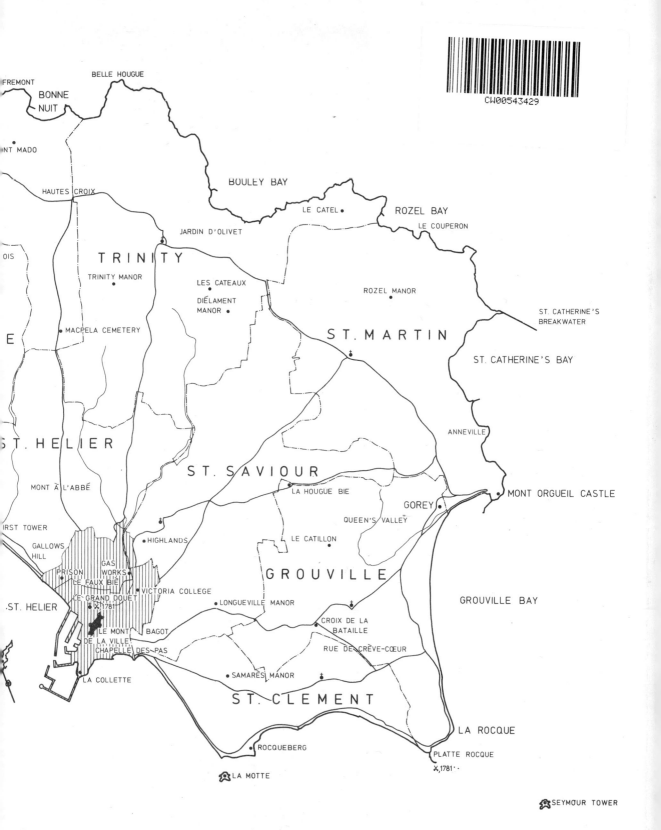

FREMONT

BONNE
NUIT

BELLE HOUGUE

NT MADO

HAUTES CROIX

BOULEY BAY

LE CATEL

ROZEL BAY

LE COUPERON

JARDIN D'OLIVET

OIS

T R I N I T Y

TRINITY MANOR

LES CATEAUX

DIÉLAMENT
MANOR

ROZEL MANOR

ST. MARTIN

ST. CATHERINE'S
BREAKWATER

MACPELA CEMETERY

E

ST. CATHERINE'S BAY

ST. HELIER

MONT À L'ABBÉ

ANNEVILLE

ST. SAVIOUR

LA HOUGUE BIE

GOREY

MONT ORGUEIL CASTLE

QUEEN'S VALLEY

IRST TOWER

GALLOWS
HILL

HIGHLANDS

LE CATILLON

GAS
WORKS
PRISON
LE FAUX BIE
LE GRAND DOUET
X 1781
VICTORIA COLLEGE

G R O U V I L L E

GROUVILLE BAY

LONGUEVILLE MANOR

.ST. HELIER

LE MONT BAGOT
DE LA VILLE
CHAPELLE DES PAS

CROIX DE LA
BATAILLE

RUE DE CRÈVE-CŒUR

LA COLLETTE

SAMARÈS MANOR

ST. CLEMENT

LA ROCQUE

ROCQUEBERG

PLATTE ROCQUE

X 1781

LA MOTTE

SEYMOUR TOWER

ICHO TOWER

BALLEINE'S HISTORY OF JERSEY

'A rugged isle, but a good nurse of noble youths; and for myself I can see nought beside sweeter than a man's own country.'

Homer. *Odyssey IX*

(*Quoted by Poingdestre, in Greek, on the title page of his* **Caesarea.**)

This revision of the original book
by G. R. Balleine is respectfully
dedicated to his memory

View across St. Aubin's Bay

'Bishop Wilberforce of Winchester came to dine at Belle Vue . . . Walked to the flagstaff with Canon Woodford, the Vicar of Leeds, and me; they said it was the loveliest view they had ever looked upon.'

From Sir John Le Couteur's diary of 5 August 1870

BALLEINE'S
HISTORY OF JERSEY

Revised and enlarged by
MARGUERITE SYVRET
and
JOAN STEVENS

PHILLIMORE

First published by
Staples Press Ltd.,
Kettering, Northamptonshire

1950

1981

Published by
PHILLIMORE & CO. LTD.
Head Office: Shopwyke Hall, Chichester,
Sussex, England

for

La Société Jersiaise,
The Museum, 9 Pier Road, St. Helier, Jersey

ISBN 0 85033 413 6

Printed in Great Britain by
THE GARDEN CITY PRESS LTD.
Letchworth, Hertfordshire, SG6 1JS

CONTENTS

LIST OF ILLUSTRATIONS

Maps

Line Drawings

FOREWORD

by

His Excellency General Sir Peter Whiteley, G.C.B., O.B.E.
(Lieutenant-Governor of Jersey)

UNLESS ONE IS DISPOSED to agree with Carlyle that 'History is a distillation of rumour' the search for fact and reason in order to establish the integrity and dignity of recorded history must be a primary aim of the historian.

The History of the Island of Jersey as originally completed by Balleine, a deeply researched and scholarly work, was, as he was the first to admit, incomplete for many reasons, not the least being the lack of contemporary records with which to fill important chapters of events. In many instances the aid of folk lore had been called in to fill the gap and to explain some of Jersey's charming idiosyncrasies.

In the 30 years which have elapsed since the original publication Joan Stevens and Marguerite Syvret have, by their diligent researches, brought in many new sources with which to verify and complement the existing work. They have moreover produced an up-to-date, expanded and eminently readable book which nevertheless retains most of the character of Balleine's original history.

To all who cherish Jersey and its people, its history, social structure, customs and traditions, and who wish for a deeper understanding of its unique constitutional position, I confidently commend this new definitive history of our Island, whether it be for historical research or simply enjoyable reading.

ACKNOWLEDGEMENTS

We are most grateful to many friends and colleagues who have helped us, and would like to mention in particular; Miss J. Arthur, Messrs. P. Bisson, S. W. Bisson, R. Cox, P. Crill (Deputy Bailiff), L. Dethan, T. Dorey, Raymond Falle, Mrs. M. Finlaison, Professor J. Le Patourel, Mrs. F. Le Sueur, Sir Robert Marett, Mr. R. Mayne, the late Professor C. McBurney, Professor A. Messervy, Mrs. M. Mimmack, Dr. A. E. Mourant, Dr. J. N. Myres, Dr. Rosemary Ommer, Messrs. V. Palmer, H. Perrée, A. Podger, the late Mr. C. G. Stevens, Senator R. Vibert.

Also the staff at the Museum of La Société Jersiaise, the Honorary Secretary Mrs. W. Macready, the Librarian, Mrs. V. Ainsworth and her helpers, Mr. J. G. Speer and Mr. R. Long of the Publications Committee. We have also consulted the officers of the States and Judicial Greffe, the Chamber of Commerce and the Methodist Archives. We have corresponded with Garter King of Arms and the Huguenot Society of London.

We are very grateful to the States Education and Tourism Committees for their encouragement and financial support.

We thank Richard Le Sueur for most of the line drawings and the maps, and most particularly Mr. Maurice Richardson, then President of La Société, who as an expert photographer has co-operated with us by taking many of the photographs used to illustrate the book, and by making copies for our use of existing prints and pictures. Photographs taken by others all carry their own acknowledgements.

La Société Jersiaise
St. Helier
Jersey
1981

MARGUERITE SYVRET
JOAN STEVENS

PREFACE

'HAPPY is the country that has no history'. Jersey is a fortunate and happy island, yet, for so small a place, it has a long, well documented and often tempestuous history, resulting mainly from its strategic position between two erstwhile enemies. If so often in earlier times the Jerseyman appears to be cantankerous, it is perhaps because the *doléances* of the poor and the quarrels of the rich are more often recorded than the pleasanter annals of everyday life.

The late G. R. Balleine, in his foreword to the original edition of this book, pointed out the uniqueness of Jersey. Although its history has run parallel with the sister Bailiwick of Guernsey, students find a fascination in noting the differences between these very similar communities.

At the time when Mr. Balleine was collecting material for his work, the authoritative histories available for study were Poingdestre, whose *Caesarea* had been published by the Société Jersiaise, Le Geyt, Falle and Le Quesne, all long out of print. The 19th century saw a spate of guide books of varying quality, perhaps the most reliable being that of Plees. There were also some specialized books such as Hoskins' *Charles II in the Channel Islands* and Quayle's *Agriculture in Jersey*. Writing in the Annual *Bulletin* of the Société Jersiaise in 1941, during the dark days of the Occupation, Mr. Balleine stressed the need for far more research to be undertaken: 'Homes and Furniture, Dress and Ornaments, Food and Cooking, Sports and Amusements, Health and Disease, Crime and Punishment, Books and Education, Folklore and Superstition, Religion and Morals, Trade and Travel, Immigration and Emigration. When those investigations have been carried right through the centuries, then, and not till then, will it be possible for someone to write a real history of Jersey'.

Meanwhile Mr. Balleine was busy collecting material from all available sources within the Island: from the archives of the States, the Royal Court and the Ecclesiastical Court, from the Public Library and, above all, from the Library of the Société Jersiaise with its valuable collection of rare books and its priceless store of manuscript material and ancient documents, of which he was custodian for many years. From this research and from material gleaned while in England came the *Biographical Dictionary of Jersey* and the popular but scholarly *History of Jersey*, published in 1950.

Since that time, as the bibliography on page xiii will show, a great many books, many of them excellent, have been written on varied aspects of island history, but for years no definitive history of Jersey has been available for purchase. The Société Jersiaise deemed it to be part of its responsibility to good learning, to the community and to the coming generation to fill this gap and to provide a history for residents, for informed visitors to the Island and for the schools. It was hard to decide whether to start *de novo*, or whether to reprint the original work by Balleine. His work was far too good to be shelved, and none of us felt that we could equal, let alone excel it. So it was decided, with the consent of the owner of the copyright, to revise and greatly expand it to include the result of recent research, which has added to our knowledge since 1950, and to cover the post-war period up till 1980. We have also added many illustrations, mostly the work of members of La Société, and have included a list of sources for the guidance of students of our history.

The study of local history is no longer frowned upon by academics; for it is seen to be the seed from which grows the national tree. So the history of Jersey is an important study in its own right as well as furnishing a microcosm of the whole. It is the story of a people who, since 1066, have been in a unique position geographically, politically and ecclesiastically, a position that has shaped their destiny over and over again; a people friendly, hardworking, thrifty, independent and proud, proud of their island heritage and, above all, proud of their special relationship with the Crown of England, as descended from the Dukedom of Normandy.

It is with these feelings in mind that we offer to the public a book which is a tribute to the memory of G. R. Balleine and is indeed mainly his work, trusting it will commend itself to all those who seek for further knowledge of the Island and to those who, as we do, love Jersey.

BIBLIOGRAPHY

SOURCE BOOKS ON JERSEY

Cartulaire de Jersey, Guernsey, et les autres Iles Normandes (a reprint of all documents relating to the islands in the Archives of the Départment de la Manche: 1025-1698). Société Jersiaise, 1919.

Jersey Prison Board Case: Memorandum prepared for the Privy Council by W. H. V. Vernon and H. Sutton (The Appendix contains many documents that touch on the Constitution of the island from 1130). Eyre & Spottiswoode, 1893.

Documents Historiques relatifs aux Iles de la Manche tirés des archives conservées dans le Public Record Office 1199-1244. Société Jersiaise 1879.

E Rotulis Litterarum Clausarum Excerpta ad Insulas Normanniae Spectantia 1205-1327. Société Jersiaise 1893.

Ancient Petitions of the Chancery and Exchequer 1290-1454. Société Jersiaise 1902.

Rolls of the Assizes held in the Channel Islands 1309. Société Jersiaise 1905.

Extentes for 1274, 1331, 1528, 1607, 1668, and 1749. All published by Société Jersiaise.

Rapport des Commissaires de Henri VIII 1515. Société Jersiaise 1878.

Actes des Etats 1524-1800. Société Jersiaise.

Ordres du Conseil enregistrés à Jersey 1536-1867. Jersey. Printed for the States.

Discipline ecclésiastique dans les iles de la Manche de 1576 à 1597: ed. by G. E. Lee. Guernsey 1885.

Chroniques de Jersey 1585 (Edition published by A Mourant. Jersey 1858).

Chroniques du Bon Duc Louis de Bourbon. J. Cabaret d'Orville (giving an eye-witness' account of du Guesclin's raid). Paris.

Journal de Jean Chevalier 1643-51. Société Jersiaise 1906.

The Lyar Confounded. Wm. Prynne. London 1645.

Pseudo Mastix, the Lyar's Whip. Michel Lemprière and others. London 1646.

A Survey of the Channel Islands. Peter Heylin. London 1656.

Caesarea or a Discourse of the Island of Jersey. Jean Poingdestre 1682. Société Jersiaise 1889.

A Survey of the Island of Jersey. P. Dumaresq 1685. Société Jersiaise 1935.

An account of the Island of Jersey. Ph. Falle, 1st edition 1694: 2nd edition 1734: edition with notes by E. Durell 1837.

Journal de Daniel Messervy 1769-72. Société Jersiaise 1896.

A Code of Laws for the Island of Jersey. 1771.

Collection of Petitions relative to Political Differences 1779-88. Jersey 1788.

Proceedings in the Trial of Moses Corbet. London 1781.

Many references to Jersey will be found in Rymer's Fœdora 1066-1383, and in the Calendars of State Papers, specially in the volume 'Domestic Series 1625-49 Addenda'.

SOME MODERN BOOKS CONCERNING JERSEY

Ahier, Philip, Stories of Jersey's seacoasts and seamen (Huddersfield). In 3 parts.

Balleine, G. R., The Bailiwick of Jersey (Hodder and Stoughton, 1951, Revised 1970).

Balleine, G. R., A Biographical Dictionary of Jersey (Staples Press).

Balleine, G. R., The Tragedy of Philippe d'Auvergne (Phillimore, 1973).

Balleine, G. R., All for the King (Société Jersiaise, 1976).

Bisson, Sidney, Jersey, Our Island (Batchworth Press, 1950).

Bois, F. de L., The Parish Church of St. Saviour, Jersey (Phillimore, 1976).

Bois, F. de L., Walks for motorists (Frederick Warne, 1979).

Brett, C. E. B., Buildings in the town and parish of St. Helier (Ulster Architectural Heritage Society for the National Trust of Jersey, 1977).

Cottrill, D. J., Victoria College, Jersey (Phillimore, 1977).

Cruickshank, C., The German Occupation of the Channel Islands (Trustees of the Imperial War Museum, 1975).

Davies, William, Fort Regent (Published privately, 1971).

de Gruchy, G. F. B., Medieval Land Tenures (Bigwood Ltd., States Printers, 1957).

de la Croix, J., *La Ville de St. Helier* (Jersey, 1845).

de la Croix, J., *Jersey, ses antiquités, ses institutions, son histoire* (Jersey, 1859).

de la Croix, J., *Les Etats* (Jersey, 1847).

de Veulle, P. M., *Le Gouvernment particulier de Jersey* (Société Jersiaise, 1974).

Dobson, R., *The Birds of the Channel Islands* (Staples Press, 1952).

Dupont, Gustave, *Histoire du Cotentin et de ses Iles* (Caen, 1870).

Durell, Rev. E., *A Picturesque and historical Guide to the Island of Jersey* (1847).

Eagleston, A. J., *The Channel Islands under Tudor Government 1485-1642* (Cambridge University Press, 1949).

Evans, Joan, *The Unconquered Knight. A translation of de Gamez' El Vitorial* (London, 1928).

Falle, Raymond, *The Royal Court House of the Island of Jersey.*

Falle, Raymond, *A Brief history of the States of Jersey and the States chamber.*

Falle, Raymond, *The States of Jersey Libraries.* (The States of Jersey, 1965, 1968, 1971).

Havet, J., *Série Chronologique des Gardiens et Seigneurs des Iles Normandes de 1198-1461* (Paris, 1876).

Hawkes, Jacquetta, *The Archaeology of the Channel Islands, Vol. II, Jersey* (Société Jersiaise, 1937).

Hoskins, S. E., *Charles II in the Channel Islands* (London, 1854).

Inglis, H. D., *The Channel Islands* (1838).

L'Amy, J. H., *Jersey Folklore* (Jersey, 1927. Reprinted).

Le Couteur, F., *Apercu sur le cidre* (Jersey, 1806).

Le Feuvre, George, *Jèrri jadis* (Don Balleine Trust, 1973).

Le Maistre, Dr. F., *Dictionnaire Jersiais Francais* (Don Balleine Trust, 1966).

Le Maistre, Dr. F., *English-Jersey Language vocabulary*, in conjunction with A. Carré and P. M. de Veulle (Don Balleine Trust, 1972).

Lemprière, R., *Portrait of the Channel Islands* (Robert Hale, 1970).

Lemprière, R., *History of the Channel Islands* (Robert Hale, 1974).

Lemprière, R., *Customs, ceremonies and traditions of the Channel Islands* (Robert Hale, 1976).

Lemprière, R., *Buildings and memorials of the Channel Islands* (Robert Hale, 1980).

Le Patourel, J. H., *The medieval administration of the Channel Islands 1199-1399* (Oxford University Press, 1937).

Le Quesne, C., *A Constitutional History of Jersey* (Jersey, 1856).

Le Sueur, Frances, *A Natural History of Jersey* (Phillimore, 1976).

Marett, R. R., *A Jerseyman at Oxford* (Oxford 1941).

Mayne, R. H., *Old Channel Islands Silver, its makers and marks* (Jersey, 1969).

Mayne, R. H., *Mailships of the Channel Islands* (Picton Publishing, 1971).

Mayne, R. H., *Jersey through the Lens* (with Joan Stevens) (Phillimore, 1975).

Millais, Geoffroy, *Sir John Everett Millais* (Academy Editions, 1979).

Moignard, I. G., *A History of Jersey's Lifeboats* (Jersey, 1975).

Mollet, R., *A Chronology of Jersey* (Société Jersiaise, 1954).

Moore, R. D., *Methodism in the Channel Islands* (London 1952).

Nicolle, E. T., *Mont Orgueil Castle* (Jersey, 1921).

Nicolle, E. T., *The Town of St. Helier* (Société Jersiaise, 1931).

Payne, J. B., *An Armorial of Jersey* (London, 1859).

Perrot, M., *La Surprise de Jersey en 1781* (Paris, 1929).

Pocock, H. R. S., *The Memoirs of Lord Coutanche* (Phillimore, 1975).

Porter, H. R., *Lillie Langtry* (Société Jersiaise, 1973).

Quayle, T., *General View of the agriculture of Jersey* (1815).

Ragg, Rev. A., *A Popular History of Jersey* (1895).

Rybot, N. V. L., *Gorey Castle Jersey* (Official Guide).

Rybot, N. V. L., *Elizabeth Castle Jersey* (Official Guide).

Saunders, A. C., *Jean Chevalier and his times* (Jersey, 1936).

Saunders, A. C., *Jersey in the 17th, 18th & 19th centuries* (1930-1931).

Schickler, F., *Les Eglises du Refuge en Angleterre* (Paris, 1892).

Sinel, L., *The German Occupation of Jersey. A diary* (Jersey, 1946).

Shepard, H. G., *One hundred years of the Royal Jersey Agricultural and Horticultural Society* (Jersey, 1933).

Stead, J., *A Picture of Jersey* (1809).

Stevens, C. G., *A Corpus of Jersey Toponymy, dictionary and maps* (1975). Further typescripts in Société Jersiaise library.

Stevens, Joan, *Old Jersey Houses*, Vol. I (Jersey, 1965; Reprint by Phillimore, 1980).

Stevens, Joan, *Old Jersey Houses*, Vol. II (Phillimore, 1977).

Stevens, Joan, *A Short History of Jersey* (Société Jersiaise, 1972).

Tessier Yandell, J., *H.M.S. Jersey 1654-1976* (Société Jersiaise, 1977).

Turk, M. G., *The Quiet Adventurers in America* (Detroit, 1975).

Turk, M. G., *The Quiet Adventurers in Canada* (Detroit, 1979).

Wood, A. and M., *Islands in Danger* (Evans Brothers, London, 1955).

Woolmer, S. C. and Arkwright, C. H., *Pewter in the Channel Islands* (Edinburgh, 1973).

A great many relevant articles may be found in the *Annual Bulletins* of La Société Jersiaise, from 1873. Further material may be found in the *Reports* and *Transactions* of La Société Guernesiaise, the *Occasional Publications* of The Jersey Society in London and the *Bulletins* of L'Assembliée d'Jèrriais.

Chapter One

THE STONE AGE TO THE GAULS

*Look unto the rock whence ye are hewn, and to the hole of the pit
whence ye are digged.*–Isaiah, Chapter 15.

THIS BOOK IS THE STORY of man in Jersey, and so it must stretch backward in time to the earliest evidence of his presence.

Jersey was not always an island, but was joined to the continent on several occasions during the period of the earliest men. So also was Britain. We know this quite certainly from the evidence of animal remains, including those of small specialized invertebrates such as snails and freshwater organisms.

The rock we call Jersey then looked over a wide grassy plain, through which flowed the waters of the Seine and other rivers emptying into the Atlantic. From the high cliffs of Jersey, as we know it, men could look across this plain, swept by the chill wind from the northern ice-sheets, to the hill tops of the Pierres de Lecq (often called the Paternosters) and of the other more northerly Channel Islands.

The first evidence of man belongs to the Old Stone Age. Paleolithic man left traces of his occupation in La Cotte de St Brelade and La Cotte à la Chèvre.[1] The former is an extremely important site which has been excavated intermittently from 1910 to 1978. It offers evidence of human occupation in two phases over a total period of some 80,000 years, and in this fact lies its international importance, as well as the unique nature of some of the finds. La Cotte à la Chèvre, hollowed out when the sea-level, at 18 metres,[2] was higher than today, contained deposits which were excavated early in this century, when numerous stone implements were found, but few traces of animal life. Two caves at Belle Hougue,[3] in Trinity parish, were probably never occupied by man, but are important because of fossil animal bones found there. Some of the fossil shells from the cave indicate a warmer climate. The deposits belong to the last warm interval before the last Ice Age and are contemporary with the 8 metre raised beach. Particularly interesting are the bones of the red deer found there, which are those of a very small variant, *Cervus elaphus jersiensis*,[4] apparently evolved through genetic isolation leading to inbreeding. A similar phenomenon has been observed on other islands at this period, notably in the Mediterranean. There were, however, no human remains whatever found in these caves, and the Island is believed to have been uninhabited at that time, that is to say approximately between 130,000 and 75,000 years before the present.

La Cotte is a cave with two phases of occupation, each sub-divided into many sub-levels, representing two widely separated eras of occupation. It was hollowed out by marine action at some period prior to the penultimate or Rissian Glaciation. As mentioned above, Jersey became an island during the temperate interglacial periods, when the water, locked up in the great northern ice-sheets, melted and returned to the sea; it was during glacial times that the Channel Islands and Britain itself were joined to the French mainland. It was then only that human occupation took place, together

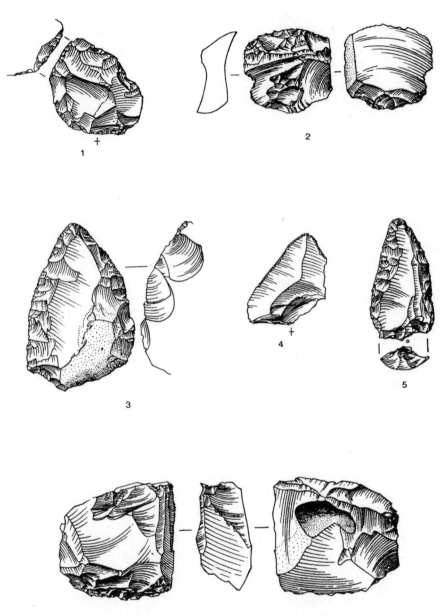

Fig. 1.   La Cotte de St. Brelade. Tools suitable for planing or scraping, from the University of Cambridge excavations. Some 130,000 years b.p. Except for no. 3, all are made by retouch on flakes and show the very extensive trimming characteristic of tools from layer A of the site.

with the presence of a rich glacial fauna which included such striking extinct species as the woolly rhinoceros and the arctic mammoth.

The evidence of the high sea levels offered by the so-called 'raised beaches' forms, nevertheless, a useful framework in which to subdivide the different periods of occupation. The latest and lowest of these beaches, recognisable throughout the Channel Islands and, under favourable conditions, in many areas of the world, reached a height of some five to eight metres above present mean sea-level. An earlier level is at 18 metres, and before that a still older one in the order of 30 metres. Between each of these the sea fell anything up to 100 metres below the present mean sea level.[5]

The earliest reliably dated human occupation is that found in the lower stage at La Cotte de St Brelade.[6] Physical readings assign it to a date of some 250,000 years ago. During the subsequent 8 metre high sea level a part of the deposit was removed by the sea which laid down instead typical beach shingle. When the sea withdrew, as the

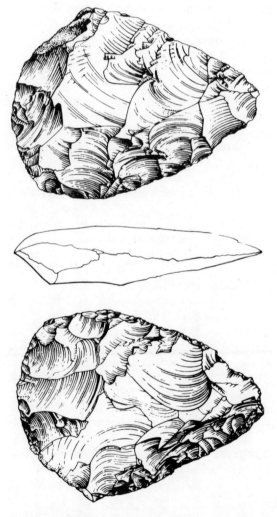

Fig. 2.   Hand axe from the Dicq. Twisted cordi-form, 98 x 72 x 21mm.

3

ice-sheets of the last glaciation advanced, the second human occupation occurred with similar traces of severe arctic cold. Five hand axes, which have been found loose at various places, are probably derived from deposits of the earlier of these two periods. They could therefore belong to a very late phase of the so-called Acheulian Period. They are of moderate workmanship, small and cordiform in outline, and are made of sea-rolled nodules of flint, while other implements are of Breton sandstone. Geological research shows that the submerged plain between Jersey and the French mainland had flint-bearing deposits now far under the sea. These would have been accessible to the inhabitants, but gradually became less available as the sea level rose. As a result the hunters were obliged to fall back on less suitable materials, some of which could be obtained locally, while some were almost certainly imported from Brittany where actual ancient quarry sites, yielding similar materials and tools of the same form, have recently been identified.

Pollen analysis has been carried out in various levels in the cave. A peaty deposit at the base of the later settlement provides evidence of ten types of tree, twenty-three of herbs and five ferns, all characteristic of the end of the last temperate (interglacial) period. Further pollen samples, obtained from the lower settlement, provide evidence of an arctic flora typical of the penultimate glaciation, and yet other samples in an intermediate position confirm this general dating.

Perhaps the most dramatic of all discoveries was made in 1910,[7] when 13 human teeth, in a good state of preservation, were found in the later occupation level. They were those of a young person of neanderthal stock, the precursor of *Homo sapiens*. The complete rhinoceros and elephant skulls found at the much lower level (penultimate glacial date) in 1970, are of equal importance. The manner in which separate piles of skull and other bones were found strongly suggests that some preparation of the meat was undertaken after the animals' death. The marked impact fractures of many of the skulls may indicate that the animals were driven over the edge of a cliff, perhaps into the cave itself.

The mammoth hunters of La Cotte finally abandoned the cave some 50,000 years ago at a time when the accumulated deposits had reached within a few feet of the roof, so that the cave was no longer habitable. No certain traces of upper paleolithic man, who left his magnificent cave paintings on the mainland of France, have been detected, and it is only recently that rare traces of his presence have been recognized in Brittany.

Scattered over the Island in various localities flint-chipping floors have also been identified, but an archaeological study of these shows that they are much later in date and belong to the post-glacial period. The flint for these may have been brought from the mainland, since we know that boats were already being made at that time, or they may have been obtained from natural erratics in the eight-metre beach, or indeed their makers may simply have walked over still dry land. These tools are suggestive of the mesolithic hunters, and, if this is so, there is a possibility that Jersey was inhabited continuously throughout these early ages.

After stormy weather peat beds and tree stumps are revealed below the beach sand in various bays, notably St Ouen's Bay. These again indicate a period of union with the continental mainland, or at least a much larger island of Jersey than at present. The predominant species among the trees were oak, beech, hazel and alder, and stumps seen from time to time denote trees of considerable size. At earliest this forest can be dated at 5,000 B.C.[8]

In about 4,000 B.C. neolithic colonists arrived, coming across Europe and up the western seaboard. They were dolichocephalic, small and comparatively civilized, making finely worked flint implements and also bows, as is proved by the many flint arrow-heads unearthed in Jersey. But most interesting of all, they were a settled people,

4

in contrast to the nomadic paleolithic man, and they discovered the advantage of growing crops and domesticating animals for food, instead of relying on hunting, with the chance fruit or root to vary their diet. In fact neolithic man was the first farmer. He learnt to grind corn to make meal, and stone querns used for this purpose are found on archaeological sites. He built huts, or perhaps true houses, made baskets, cloth and pottery. Those who settled on the Minquiers reef[9] were seal hunters, so must also have built boats. There was trade, as is shown by implements brought from afar, and particularly by the eight 'jadeite' axes of advanced workmanship, probably emanating from the Alps via Brittany.[10] Other axes are made of Grand Pressigny flint, Indre et Loire and Plussulien dolomite, and fibrolite from Brittany. These apparently warlike tools were almost certainly used principally for felling trees, working with wood and hunting small animals. 'Cup markings' on some stone monuments may be a first step towards a form of written communication.[11]

Jersey is rich in dolmens, the tombs of Stone Age man. The word is Breton and means *dol*, a table, and *men* a stone. In their simplest form they consist of two upright stones with a capstone laid across them. They are often erroneously referred to as Druids' temples, but they pre-date the Druids (of whom there is no clear evidence in Jersey) by many centuries. There are seven major dolmens, Faldouet in St Martin, Mont Ubé in St Clement, Les Monts Grantez in St Ouen, Le Couperon in St Martin, two in First Tower Park and one now buried in the peat beneath the Gas Works site in town. But the most outstanding example is La Hougue Bie[12] in Grouville, where a mound 13 metres high covers a spectacular example of a neolithic passage grave. Pottery was found within and the bones of eight persons, three of them women. There used to be many more of what are locally called *pouquelayes*, for Poingdestre, writing in 1682, speaks of 'half a hundred.' One (perhaps two) stood on Le Mont de la Ville, above the town and was discovered in 1785. It obstructed the levelling of a military parade ground and was given to the then Governor, Marshal Conway, who had taken a great interest in its discovery. He conveyed it to his home, Park Place, near Henley, where it may still be seen.[13] The frequent occurrence of the word *hougue* (a mound) and *pouquelaye* (a dolmen) in documents and in place names is evidence of the many monuments which have at some time existed.

The tombs, dating from about 4,000 B.C., may have been erected for important people only, such as tribal chiefs, and they presuppose a population able to drag the immense blocks of stone from distant beaches and other sites, to erect these monuments and then to cover them with earth. At La Hougue Bie, for instance, there are 69 large stones, some weighing about 30 ton, brought uphill from considerable distances. It has even been suggested, perhaps fancifully, that this is the origin of the name *La Rue Crève-Coeur* (Heartbreak Road) which leads to La Hougue Bie across the spine of the Grouville Hills.

The fair number of menhirs, or standing stones, are clearly man's work; often they are not of the stone of the locality in which they are found, and on excavation they are seen to have 'trig stones' to support them at their base. Many have been moved or broken up for building material. Whether they were intended for worship or for some ritualistic purpose, we do not know.

Jersey remained inhabited by the neolithic peoples for about 1,300 years, a period long enough to leave time for developments which cannot be traced in detail. It is known that early in this period England and Northern France were invaded by the Beaker folk, warlike tribes named from a distinctive type of drinking vessel which they used. Fragments of 16 of their beakers, as well as many sherds, have been found in the Island, 12 of them in the passage grave at First Tower, which must therefore have been an important tomb; only four have been found elsewhere.

Fig. 3.   The gold torque, before repair done by the British Museum. Drawn from an early photo-
graph. Bronze Age.

The Bronze Age is sometimes thought of as a new type of civilization, but it was not so in Jersey. When wandering smiths of the metal-workers' craft reached our shores, some of the rich no doubt invested in this wonderful new metal; but the mass of the people continued to use flint or stone implements. One particularly important chief brought to the island the magnificent torque, owned by La Société Jersiaise, which workmen found in 1889 when digging foundations for a house in St Helier.[14] It is composed of 140 centimetres of gold, twisted into a four-flanged spiral bar. It weighs 746 grammes and is of Irish origin: similar, but smaller, torques have been found in Wales, England, Brittany and Normandy. None can say to whom it belonged nor exactly whence it came. Nor can we be sure of its purpose, but it must surely have been some sort of human adornment. Evidence of the Bronze Age is present in Jersey, and some hoards of implements have been found. The most notable collection was one of 110 items, unearthed in 1976,[15] consisting of a pottery jar containing weapons, mostly spears and swords, perhaps the stock in trade of an itinerant smith as mentioned above. This hoard was found in St Lawrence, but it is possible that Jersey's acid soil has destroyed much Bronze Age material, which would otherwise have been more plentiful.

Life for the inhabitants was not always peaceful. The cracked sling-stone found inside the Iron Age village at the Pinnacle, and arrow-heads with their tips broken, suggest that on some occasion there was a severe assault here. In another village site at Blanches Banques was found a cooking pot, still upright and half-filled with limpet shells, suggesting that the inhabitants had had to flee for their lives and had never returned. But of inter-tribal wars we know nothing; a pity, as one would greatly like to know more of these swarthy folk, who must be the ancestors of some of our present day population.

But a time of great change and further invasion was looming. In the forests of Central Europe the tribes were again stirring, and wave after wave of tall, fair-haired, blue-eyed warriors began to pour up the Danube, across France and up to Normandy and Brittany, though they had not yet assumed these names. These were the Iron Age Celts, or Gauls, who enter history in about 800 B.C.

At intervals in the story of man, some discovery has been so fundamental as to alter the future of the world. One was that fire could warm us and cook our food, perhaps the greatest discovery of all and the one which to a great extent separates man from the apes. Another was the motive power of the wheel; another, centuries later, was the printing press. The Celts, in their time, were irresistible, as they had discovered iron, which gave them weapons that were invincible; they also introduced into Western Europe and domesticated the horse, and this made them mobile. About 300 B.C. one of these tribes, the Coriosolites, conquered the Cotentin (the peninsula due east of the islands) and subjugated that part of Normandy and apparently the off-shore island of Jersey also. It is questionable whether they came to Jersey permanently or temporarily, but in either case, with their superior strength, they would have conquered the indigenous population. Intermarriage, the inevitable result of a conquest, would further have established their dominance.[16]

These Iron Age men came of a race new to these latitudes: they had a culture, language and religion that were all foreign. They brought with them a more advanced degree of civilization, and in France (though not in Jersey) they have left inscriptions which cannot as yet be interpreted. They loved music, particularly the harp; with iron saws, hammers and nails they built timber houses; with bill-hooks, axes and spades they brought the land under cultivation; they controlled preying animals and grew wheat, barley, oats and rye, as well as beans; but they fed principally on meat and drank a form of barley beer. They had oak ships with skin sails, clumsy to handle, but so strong that the Romans found it impossible to sink them. Their government was

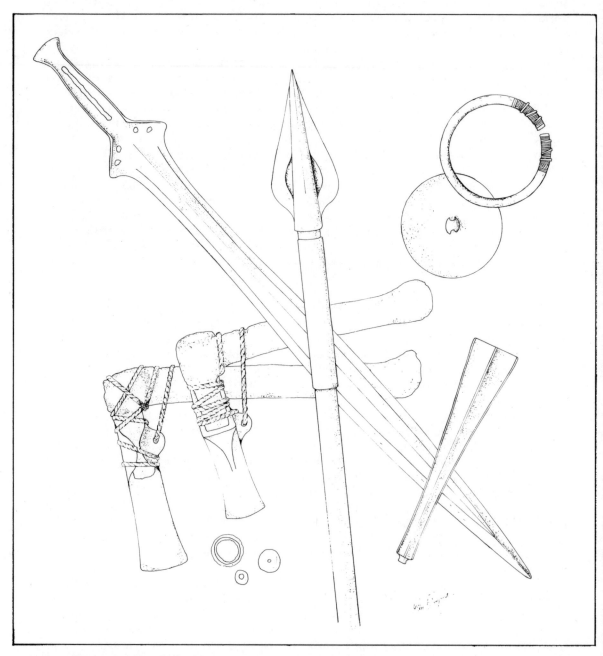

Fig. 4.   An artist's impression of items from the late Bronze Age hoard discovered in St. Lawrence in 1976.
c. 1,000 BC.

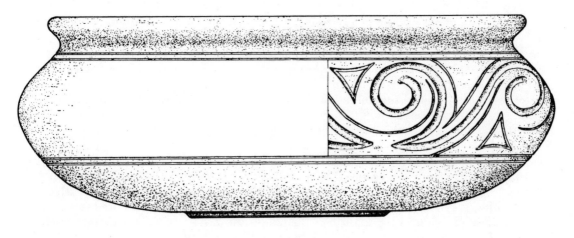

A.B.

Fig. 5.   Early Iron Age bowl, La Tène culture, dated 3rd century BC. Diameter at lip 26cm.
Uncovered during a rescue excavation in Broad Street, St. Helier.

autocratic, with the Chief supreme in his tribe, and the father in his family, with power
of life and death. It is interesting to speculate whether it was the power of iron, in
implements of war and peace, which made them so belligerent. Which was cause and
which effect? We can only surmise to what extent they affected life in Jersey.

Each tribal chief coined his own money. The Greeks had established a colony at
Marseilles, which used Philip of Macedon's coins with the head of Apollo on one side
and on the reverse Philip's chariot winning the Olympic crown. These were copied

Fig. 6.   Obverse and reverse of a typical coin from the Armorican
hoards, 1st century BC.

and adapted, and thousands of examples, with their striking designs, have been dug up in Jersey on several sites, notably La Marquanderie in St Brelade, Le Câtel at Rozel and le Câtillon at Grouville. They vary from near copies to almost unrecognisable stylisations. They can be closely dated to 53–50 B.C. and are of copper/tin/silver alloy. Our examples come from the Coriosolites and appear to be the accumulated wealth of Gauls fleeing from the advancing Romans and taking refuge in this remote island, which they thought might offer some security for their life's capital savings.[17]

A striking feature in the life of these Gauls was their bloodthirsty religion. The Romans declared that no race on earth was so fantastically religious. Their white-robed, college-trained priesthood of Druids, with a 20 years' noviciate, was the powerful unifying bond between the tribes. The Druids had no temples, but built altars in the open air, on hill tops or in sacred groves. To the old worship of the Earth Mother, almost universal in pre-historic times (two images of her survive in Guernsey), they added a sky-god, whom they made her husband, and a host of nature deities, such as Borvo, god of the hot springs, Vosegus, god of the forests, and Taranis, god of thunder.[18] And they worshipped them with human sacrifices, who were burnt alive. The old customs could not survive against this fierce, fanatical faith, and no more dolmens were built. In a couple of generations the descendants of the dolmen builders had forgotten their old ways, and presumably the Island, like the mainland, adopted the gods of the Gauls.

Many descriptions of these Gauls have come down to us from classical texts. Strabo, a Greek historian and geographer of the 1st century A.D., tells us that the race was 'madly fond of war, high-spirited and quick to battle, but otherwise straightforward and not of evil character. . . . To the frankness and high-spiritedness of their temperament must be added the traits of childish boastfulness and love of decoration. They wear ornaments of gold, torques on their necks and bracelets on their arms and wrists, while people of high rank wear dyed garments besprinkled with gold'.[19] Today modern archaeological discoveries are deepening our knowledge of the Celtic race to which they belonged, and whose influence was felt throughout Europe from the borders of Scythia[20] to the western shores of Brittany and Ireland. The dominance of these Celtic people lasted for five centuries, but in 56 B.C. they in their turn were conquered by the Romans.